Trek to the Top

by Megan McDonald

PEARSON

Scott
Foresman

Editorial Offices: Glenview, Illinois • Parsippany, New Jersey • New York, New York
Sales Offices: Needham, Massachusetts • Duluth, Georgia • Glenview, Illinois
Coppell, Texas • Ontario, California • Mesa, Arizona

ISBN: 0-328-13243-8

7 8 9 10 V010 14 13 12 11 10 09 08

When you look at Earth, you see both water and land. Bodies of water include rivers, oceans, lakes, ponds, and seas.

The features and shapes of the land are called **landforms.** There are many kinds of landforms, such as mountains, plains, hills, and valleys.

Let's take a closer look at land and water.

3

Oceans

Most of Earth is covered by water. An ocean is the largest body of water on Earth. Oceans hold most of Earth's water supply. There are four main oceans. They are the Atlantic Ocean, Pacific Ocean, Arctic Ocean, and Indian Ocean. These four oceans are all connected. Oceans have salty water.

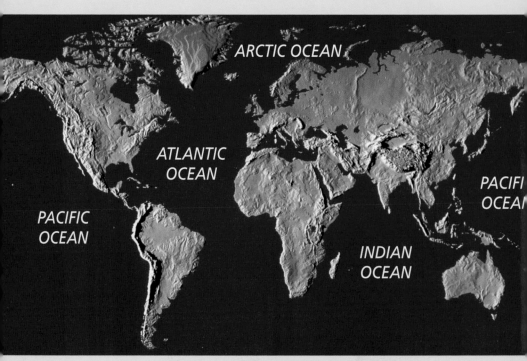

The world and its oceans

Seas, Gulfs, and Bays

Seas are also large bodies of salt water. Seas are smaller than oceans. Some seas are connected to oceans. Seas are partly or almost completely closed in by land.

Gulfs and bays are similar to seas, but smaller. Gulfs or bays are formed when parts of the sea or ocean reach into land. They are mostly surrounded by land on the sides. Gulfs are larger than bays.

Lakes and Ponds

A lake is a large body of water surrounded by land on all sides. Lakes have fresh water. They are not salty.

A pond is a small body of water surrounded by land. Ponds are smaller than lakes. Ponds also have freshwater.

A pond in Australia

Rivers

Rivers are large, flowing bodies of water. Rivers have fresh water. Most rivers flow into an even larger body of water. They could flow into an ocean, a sea, or a big lake. The end of a river, where it meets an ocean, sea, or lake, is called the river's mouth.

Some rivers are very long. The longest river in the world is the Nile River. It is more than four thousand miles long! The Nile River is in Africa. It flows into the Mediterranean Sea.

The Nile River

The Water Cycle

Bodies of water and landforms work together in Earth's water cycle. As the picture shows, water evaporates from water and land. It goes into the air as a gas called water vapor and forms clouds.

The clouds blow toward the high mountains. The mountains cool the air, and rain or snow falls to the ground. This is called **precipitation.** The water from the rain or snow runs into rivers that carve valleys and water the plains.

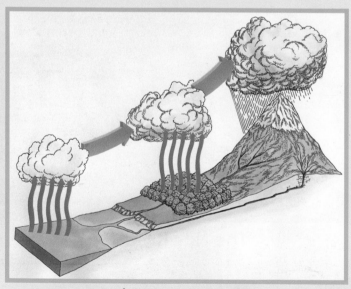

Earth's water cycle

Mountains

Mountains are important landforms. Mountains are made up of rocky land. They have steep sides and a pointed or rounded top. Mountains are the tallest parts of Earth. They can form when the crust of Earth moves or lava breaks through the crust.

Mountains can even be found under Earth's oceans. Some islands are the tops of mountains peeking out of the water.

Mount Everest is the highest point on Earth.

Valleys

Valleys are low places between mountains and hills. The bottom of a valley is called the valley's floor. The valley floor usually has very fertile soil, so it is good for farmland. The valley's sides are called valley walls or valley slopes. Some valleys are very narrow and have steep sides. These valleys are called **canyons.**

The Grand Canyon

Plains

Some places on Earth are almost flat. Plains are flat or gently rolling areas. Dry plains can be covered in grass. These are called grasslands. Other plains where there is more **moisture** can be covered in trees.

The Great Plains

Desert Forms

Deserts are places that do not get much rain. Deserts are very **arid,** or dry. Many deserts are covered with rocks, stones, or sand. Look at the tall rocks in the photo below. There is not a lot of tall plant life in deserts to stop the wind from shaping these landforms. These rock landforms are called buttes.

Monument Valley in Arizona is a desert with rock landforms.

There are many different kinds of landforms and bodies of water on Earth. Mountains, valleys, oceans, lakes, and rivers are all important parts of Earth. As you read books, see movies, or drive around, look for landforms and waterways. How do they affect what you read, see, or feel?

Now Try This

Land and Water Game

You and a friend can have fun and learn more about Earth's landforms and bodies of water by making and playing this game.

You can play this game using only the landforms and bodies of water mentioned in the book, or you can make the game more interesting by trying to find pictures of land or water not included here.

Here's How to Do It!

You will need old magazines or travel brochures that you can cut up, or pictures off the Internet. You will also need scissors, glue or paste, writing paper, and two boxes or bags for putting the pictures in.

1. Find as many pictures as you can of landforms and bodies of water, and cut them out.

2. Glue your pictures to sheets of paper, one picture to a page.

3. You and your partner each put your pictures in a different box or bag. Take turns pulling out each other's pictures, and try to name the landform or body of water shown.

4. You could also pull out a picture and try to describe the landform or body of water in words. See if your partner can guess its name from your description.

Glossary

arid *adj.* very dry.

canyons *n.* deep, narrow valleys with steep sides.

landforms *n.* features that make up Earth's surface, such as mountains or valleys.

moisture *n.* wetness.

precipitation *n.* rain or snow that falls to Earth's surface.